Symphonies Nos. 1 and 2

in Full Score

Edward Elgar

DOVER PUBLICATIONS, INC.
Mineola, New York

Bibliographical Note

This Dover edition, first published in 1999, is a new compilation of two works originally published separately by Novello and Company, Limited, London: *Symphony* [No. 1] *for Full Orchestra / Composed by Edward Elgar (Op. 55)*, 1908; and *Symphony No. 2 (in E Flat) for Full Orchestra . . . (Op. 63)*, 1911.
The Shelley quotation on p. 171 is reproduced as it appeared in the original edition. A facsimile of the original dedication page of Symphony No. 2 is reproduced on p. 172. Both instrumentation lists are newly added.

International Standard Book Number: 0-486-40855-8

Manufactured in the United States of America
Dover Publications, Inc., 31 East 2nd Street, Mineola, N.Y. 11501

CONTENTS

To Hans Richter, Mus. Doc.
True artist and true friend

Symphony No. 1
in A-flat major

Op. 55 (1907–8)

INSTRUMENTATION

3 Flutes [Flauto, Fl.]
    Fl. III doubles Piccolo [Picc.]
2 Oboes [Oboi, Ob.]
English Horn [Corno Inglese, C. Ingl.]
2 Clarinets in A, B♭ [Clarinetti, Cl.]
Bass Clarinet in A, B♭ [Clarinetto Basso, Cl. B(asso)]
2 Bassoons [Fagotti, Fag.]
Contrabassoon [Contra Fagotto, C. Fag.]

4 Horns in F [Corni, Cor.]
3 Trumpets in B♭ [Trombe, Tr.]
3 Trombones [Tromboni, Trb.]
Tuba [Tuba, Tb.]

Timpani

Percussion
    Small Snare Drum [Tamburo piccolo, T. picc.]
    Bass Drum & Cymbals [Gran Cassa & Piatti,
        Gr.C. & Piat.]

Violins I, II [Violini, Vio.]
Violas [Viole]
Cellos [Violoncelli, Vcl.]
Basses [Contra Bassi, C.B.]

I.

III.

IV.

137

Symphony No. 2
in E-flat major
Op. 63 (1909–11)

"RARELY, RARELY COMEST THOU,
SPIRIT OF DELIGHT!"

Shelley

Dedicated
to the Memory of
His late Majesty
King Edward VII.

———

This Symphony designed early in 1910 to be a loyal
tribute, bears its present dedication with the gracious
approval of His Majesty the King.

March 16th 1911.

INSTRUMENTATION

3 Flutes [Flauto, Fl.]
    Fl. III doubles Piccolo [Picc.]
2 Oboes [Oboi, Ob.]
English Horn [Corno Inglese, C. Ingl.]
Clarinet in E♭[Clarinetto, Cl.]
2 Clarinets in B♭[Clarinetti, Cl.]
Bass Clarinet in B♭[Clarinetto Basso, Cl. B(asso)]
2 Bassoons [Fagotti, Fag.]
Contrabassoon [Contra Fagotto, C. Fag.]

4 Horns in F [Corni, Cor.]
3 Trumpets in B♭[Trombe, Tr.]
3 Trombones [Tromboni, Trb.]
Tuba [Tuba, Tb.]

Timpani

Percussion
    Small Snare Drum [Tamburo piccolo, T. picc.]
        & Tambourine [Tamburino, Tamb.]
    Bass Drum & Cymbals [Gran Cassa & Piatti,
        Gr.C. & Piat.]

Violins I, II [Violini, Vio.]
Violas [Viole]
Cellos [Violoncelli, Vcl.]
Basses [Contra Bassi, C.B.]

I.

Major/minor

Second theme
in G minor

34

IV.

145 Poco animato.

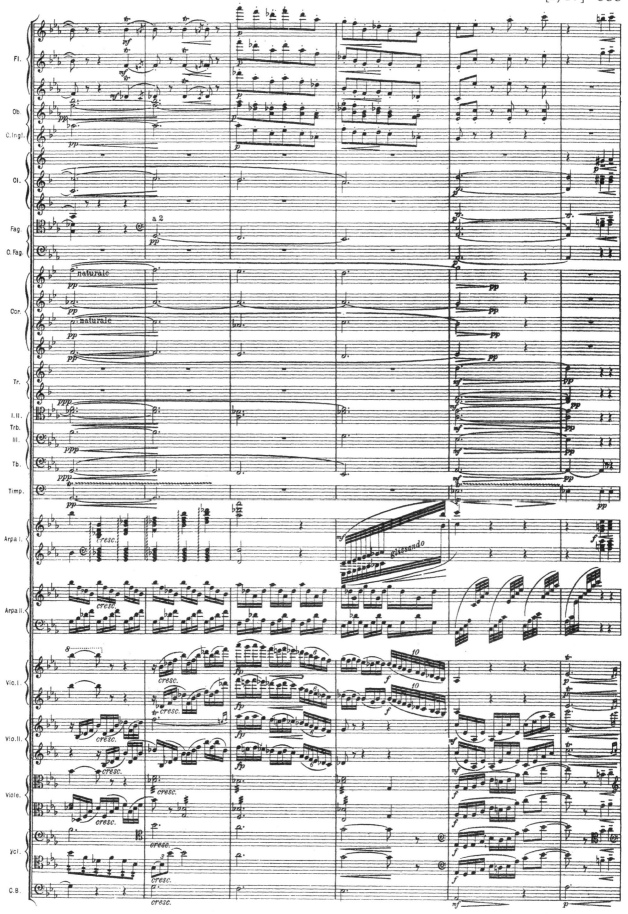

Venice - Tintagel (1910 - 11)

END OF EDITION

Dover Orchestral Scores

Bach, Johann Sebastian, COMPLETE CONCERTI FOR SOLO KEYBOARD AND ORCHESTRA IN FULL SCORE. Bach's seven complete concerti for solo keyboard and orchestra in full score from the authoritative Bach-Gesellschaft edition. 206pp. 9 x 12. 24929-8

Bach, Johann Sebastian, THE SIX BRANDENBURG CONCERTOS AND THE FOUR ORCHESTRAL SUITES IN FULL SCORE. Complete standard Bach-Gesellschaft editions in large, clear format. Study score. 273pp. 9 x 12. 23376-6

Bach, Johann Sebastian, THE THREE VIOLIN CONCERTI IN FULL SCORE. Concerto in A Minor, BWV 1041; Concerto in E Major, BWV 1042; and Concerto for Two Violins in D Minor, BWV 1043. Bach-Gesellschaft editions. 64pp. 9⅜ x 12¼. 25124-1

Beethoven, Ludwig van, COMPLETE PIANO CONCERTOS IN FULL SCORE. Complete scores of five great Beethoven piano concertos, with all cadenzas as he wrote them, reproduced from authoritative Breitkopf & Härtel edition. New Table of Contents. 384pp. 9⅜ x 12¼. 24563-2

Beethoven, Ludwig van, SIX GREAT OVERTURES IN FULL SCORE. Six staples of the orchestral repertoire from authoritative Breitkopf & Härtel edition. *Leonore Overtures,* Nos. 1–3; Overtures to *Coriolanus, Egmont, Fidelio.* 288pp. 9 x 12. 24789-9

Beethoven, Ludwig van, SYMPHONIES NOS. 1, 2, 3, AND 4 IN FULL SCORE. Republication of H. Litolff edition. 272pp. 9 x 12. 26033-X

Beethoven, Ludwig van, SYMPHONIES NOS. 5, 6 AND 7 IN FULL SCORE, Ludwig van Beethoven. Republication of H. Litolff edition. 272pp. 9 x 12. 26034-8

Beethoven, Ludwig van, SYMPHONIES NOS. 8 AND 9 IN FULL SCORE. Republication of H. Litolff edition. 256pp. 9 x 12. 26035-6

Beethoven, Ludwig van; Mendelssohn, Felix; and Tchaikovsky, Peter Ilyitch, GREAT ROMANTIC VIOLIN CONCERTI IN FULL SCORE. The Beethoven Op. 61, Mendelssohn Op. 64 and Tchaikovsky Op. 35 concertos reprinted from Breitkopf & Härtel editions. 224pp. 9 x 12. 24989-1

Brahms, Johannes, COMPLETE CONCERTI IN FULL SCORE. Piano Concertos Nos. 1 and 2; Violin Concerto, Op. 77; Concerto for Violin and Cello, Op. 102. Definitive Breitkopf & Härtel edition. 352pp. 9⅜ x 12¼. 24170-X

Brahms, Johannes, COMPLETE SYMPHONIES. Full orchestral scores in one volume. No. 1 in C Minor, Op. 68; No. 2 in D Major, Op. 73; No. 3 in F Major, Op. 90; and No. 4 in E Minor, Op. 98. Reproduced from definitive Vienna Gesellschaft der Musikfreunde edition. Study score. 344pp. 9 x 12. 23053-8

Brahms, Johannes, THREE ORCHESTRAL WORKS IN FULL SCORE: Academic Festival Overture, Tragic Overture and Variations on a Theme by Joseph Haydn. Reproduced from the authoritative Breitkopf & Härtel edition three of Brahms's great orchestral favorites. Editor's commentary in German and English. 112pp. 9⅜ x 12¼. 24637-X

Chopin, Frédéric, THE PIANO CONCERTOS IN FULL SCORE. The authoritative Breitkopf & Härtel full-score edition in one volume; Piano Concertos No. 1 in E Minor and No. 2 in F Minor. 176pp. 9 x 12. 25835-1

Corelli, Arcangelo, COMPLETE CONCERTI GROSSI IN FULL SCORE. All 12 concerti in the famous late nineteenth-century edition prepared by violinist Joseph Joachim and musicologist Friedrich Chrysander. 240pp. 8⅜ x 11¼. 25606-5

Debussy, Claude, THREE GREAT ORCHESTRAL WORKS IN FULL SCORE. Three of the Impressionist's most-recorded, most-performed favorites: *Prélude à l'Après-midi d'un Faune, Nocturnes,* and *La Mer.* Reprinted from early French editions. 279pp. 9 x 12. 24441-5

Dvořák, Antonín, SERENADE NO. 1, OP. 22, AND SERENADE NO. 2, OP. 44, IN FULL SCORE. Two works typified by elegance of form, intense harmony, rhythmic variety, and uninhibited emotionalism. 96pp. 9 x 12. 41895-2

Dvořák, Antonín, SYMPHONY NO. 8 IN G MAJOR, OP. 88, SYMPHONY NO. 9 IN E MINOR, OP. 95 ("NEW WORLD") IN FULL SCORE. Two celebrated symphonies by the great Czech composer, the Eighth and the immensely popular Ninth, "From the New World," in one volume. 272pp. 9 x 12. 24749-X

Elgar, Edward, CELLO CONCERTO IN E MINOR, OP. 85, IN FULL SCORE. A tour de force for any cellist, this frequently performed work is widely regarded as an elegy for a lost world. Melodic and evocative, it exhibits a remarkable scope, ranging from tragic passion to buoyant optimism. Reproduced from an authoritative source. 112pp. 8⅜ x 11. 41896-0

Franck, César, SYMPHONY IN D MINOR IN FULL SCORE. Superb, authoritative edition of Franck's only symphony, an often-performed and recorded masterwork of late French romantic style. 160pp. 9 x 12. 25373-2

Handel, George Frideric, COMPLETE CONCERTI GROSSI IN FULL SCORE. Monumental Opus 6 Concerti Grossi, Opus 3 and "Alexander's Feast" Concerti Grossi—19 in all—reproduced from the most authoritative edition. 258pp. 9⅜ x 12¼. 24187-4

Handel, George Frideric, GREAT ORGAN CONCERTI, OPP. 4 & 7, IN FULL SCORE. 12 organ concerti composed by the great Baroque master are reproduced in full score from the Deutsche Handelgesellschaft edition. 138pp. 9⅜ x 12¼. 24462-8

Handel, George Frideric, WATER MUSIC AND MUSIC FOR THE ROYAL FIREWORKS IN FULL SCORE. Full scores of two of the most popular Baroque orchestral works performed today—reprinted from the definitive Deutsche Handelgesellschaft edition. Total of 96pp. 8⅛ x 11. 25070-9

Haydn, Joseph, SYMPHONIES 88–92 IN FULL SCORE: The Haydn Society Edition. Full score of symphonies Nos. 88 through 92. Large, readable noteheads, ample margins for fingerings, etc., and extensive Editor's Commentary. 304pp. 9 x 12. (Available in U.S. only) 24445-8

Liszt, Franz, THE PIANO CONCERTI IN FULL SCORE. Here in one volume are Piano Concerto No. 1 in E-flat Major and Piano Concerto No. 2 in A Major—among the most studied, recorded, and performed of all works for piano and orchestra. 144pp. 9 x 12. 25221-3

Mahler, Gustav, DAS LIED VON DER ERDE IN FULL SCORE. Mahler's masterpiece, a fusion of song and symphony, reprinted from the original 1912 Universal Edition. English translations of song texts. 160pp. 9 x 12. 25657-X

Mahler, Gustav, SYMPHONIES NOS. 1 AND 2 IN FULL SCORE. Unabridged, authoritative Austrian editions of Symphony No. 1 in D Major ("Titan") and Symphony No. 2 in C Minor ("Resurrection"). 384pp. 8⅛ x 11. 25473-9

Mahler, Gustav, SYMPHONIES NOS. 3 AND 4 IN FULL SCORE. Two brilliantly contrasting masterworks—one scored for a massive ensemble, the other for small orchestra and soloist—reprinted from authoritative Viennese editions. 368pp. 9⅜ x 12¼. 26166-2